Food Webs

Lisa Greathouse

Consultant

Sterling Vamvas
Chemist, Orange County
Water District

Image Credits: p.24 (bottom left); Christina
Kennedy/Alamy; p.7 (bottom right) Juniors
Bildarchiv GmbH/Alamy; p.11 (bottom right) Rolf
Nussbaumer Photography/Alamy; pp.5–7, 12, 15–17
(illustrations) Tim Bradley; p.22 AFP/Getty Images;
p.23 National Geographic Creative/Getty Images;
pp.18–21 (illustrations) Travis Hanson; p.32 Megan
Iatzko; pp.28–29 (illustrations) J.J. Rudisill; backcover,
pp.4 (left), 4–5 (background), 6 (middle right), 7 (top
right), 6–7 (background), 8 (left) 8–9 (background),
10–11 (background), 15 (center left, right, top right),
16 (top, right, & left), 17 (top), 16–17 (background),
21 (right), 22 (top & background), 24 (bottom right),
26–27 (background), 31 iStock; all other images
from Shutterstock.

Library of Congress Cataloging-in-Publication Data

Greathouse, Lisa E., author.
  Food webs / Lisa Greathouse.
    pages cm
  Summary: "A snail eats a leaf. A bird eats the snail. A cat
eats the bird. Living things need one another to survive.
This is how a food web works. Even you are part of a
food web! What did you eat for breakfast this morning?
Find out where you fit into the food web by opening this
book"—Provided by publisher.
  Audience: K to grade 3.
  Includes index.
  ISBN 978-1-4807-4638-1 (pbk.)
  ISBN 1-4807-4638-X (pbk.)
  ISBN 978-1-4807-5082-1 (ebook)
  1. Food chains (Ecology)—Juvenile literature.
  2. Biotic communities—Juvenile literature. I. Title.
  QH541.15.F66G74 2015
  577.16—dc23
                              2014034229

Teacher Created Materials

5301 Oceanus Drive
Huntington Beach, CA 92649-1030
http://www.tcmpub.com
ISBN 978-1-4807-4638-1

Table of Contents

If It's Alive, It Needs Energy

Is it lunchtime yet? By the time the lunch bell rings, you are probably hungry. That's because your body needs **energy** to get through the day. The energy you get from the food you eat helps you run at recess. It helps you focus while you're doing homework. It helps you fight off the flu and other illnesses. The energy from the food you eat even keeps your heart beating and your blood pumping.

In other words, you couldn't live without energy from food. The same is true for all living things on Earth. All living plants and animals need energy to live. Plants get their energy from air, soil, water, and the sun. Animals get their energy by eating plants and other animals. That flow of energy from one living thing to another is called a *food chain*. A food chain branches out to many animals. As it grows, it starts to look like a web—a food web!

SUN

ENERGY

PLANT

4

SNAKE

ENERGY

HAWK

ENERGY

ENERGY

ENERGY

ENERGY

RAT

ENERGY

GRASSHOPPER

ENERGY

Passing Along Energy

This is an example of a basic food web. It shows the flow of energy from the sun to a plant to a bug to a rat to a snake to a hawk. But the bug and rat can also be food for the hawk.

Food webs show how animals get energy from other **organisms**. They show who eats who. They are a simple way to understand a complex process. It may be difficult to see how a plant in one place gives energy to an animal far away. But a food web can show how they connect.

There are many types of food webs. They vary based on the part of the world you are in. You wouldn't see an African lion or a polar bear in an American food web—except at the zoo! A food web from Greece might have olives, goats, and bears in it. A food web from China might have grass, birds, and alligators. Wherever they are from, food webs show how **species** relate.

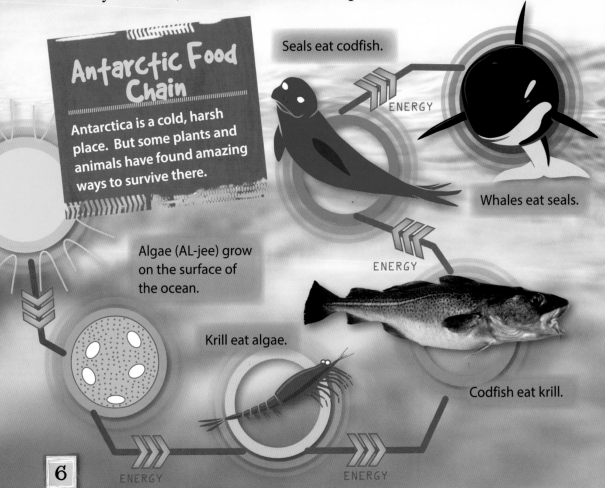

Antarctic Food Chain

Antarctica is a cold, harsh place. But some plants and animals have found amazing ways to survive there.

Seals eat codfish.

Whales eat seals.

Algae (AL-jee) grow on the surface of the ocean.

Krill eat algae.

Codfish eat krill.

ENERGY

ENERGY

ENERGY

ENERGY

ENERGY

North American Food Chain

North America is home to many different types of plants and animals. This is one example of a food chain in North America.

A plant gets energy from the sun and the soil.

ENERGY

A cougar eats the fox.

ENERGY

A grasshopper eats the plant.

ENERGY

A fox eats the mouse.

A mouse eats the grasshopper.

ENERGY

Plants Are Producers

All food webs start with the sun. The sun provides plants with the energy they need to grow. And plants provide energy to billions of animals around the world.

Plants use air, sunlight, water, and soil to make their own food. That's why plants are known as **producers** in a food web. There are a lot of links in a food web. But plants are some of the only creatures that directly use the sun's energy to make food.

Producers of the Ocean

Plants aren't the only producers. Some tiny creatures that live in the ocean, such as algae, also make their own food from the sun's energy.

There are over 20,000 known types of algae.

Parts of a Plant

Every part of a plant has a job. The roots, stem, and leaves all contribute to the plant's survival.

The leaves take in light to make food.

The stem holds up the plant.

The roots take in nutrients and water.

Animals Are Consumers

Animals that eat plants are the next link in a food web. They use energy from plants to grow and live. Animals that eat only plants are called **herbivores**. In a food web, they are called **primary consumers**.

Primary consumers can be small animals. Insects or rabbits are primary consumers. But there are also large herbivores. These include giraffes, elephants, and bison (BAHY-suhn).

Bison normally eat five times a day!

Chewing the Cud

Many primary consumers have special features to help them eat plants, which can be hard to chew and digest. Wide teeth help them grind up leaves and grasses. Special stomachs help them break down and digest plants.

Predator or Prey?

Animals that eat other animals are called *predators*. The animals they eat are their *prey*.

Most primary consumers are small animals that are eaten by larger animals. When a cricket eats a leaf, it is a primary consumer. Then, along comes something bigger, such as a mouse, which eats the cricket. That mouse is a **secondary consumer**. The energy the cricket gets from the plant moves to the mouse. A tertiary consumer, perhaps a bird, may then eat the secondary consumer. The energy goes from the sun to plants. Then, it moves from one animal to the next.

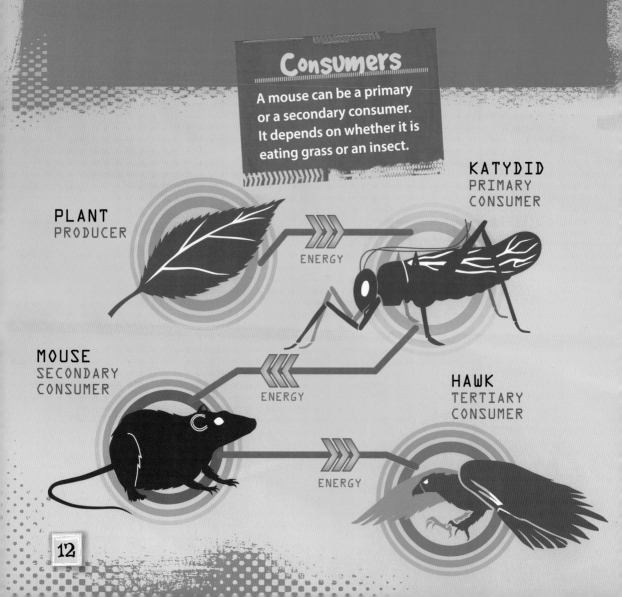

Consumers

A mouse can be a primary or a secondary consumer. It depends on whether it is eating grass or an insect.

KATYDID
PRIMARY
CONSUMER

PLANT
PRODUCER

ENERGY

MOUSE
SECONDARY
CONSUMER

HAWK
TERTIARY
CONSUMER

ENERGY

ENERGY

Hungry?

Life in a food web is classified by how things get energy. What kind of consumer are you? Find out!

Do you eat meat?

NO You're a herbivore. You eat only plants.

YES Do you eat anything else?

NO You're a **carnivore**. You eat only animals.

YES You're an **omnivore**. You eat both plants and animals.

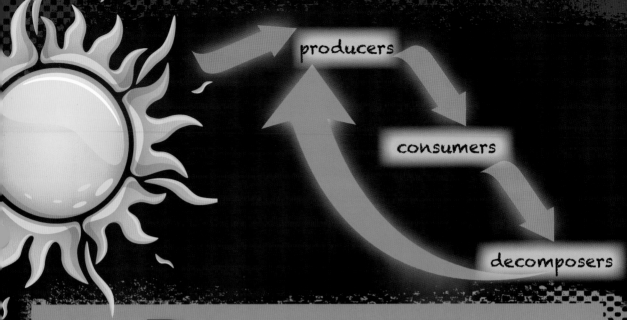

producers

consumers

decomposers

Decomposers Do the Dirty Work

What happens when a powerful animal eats another animal? Is that the end of the food chain? Not by a long shot! At some point, that animal is going to die. That's when **scavengers** and **decomposers** start their work.

Have you ever seen a dead animal in the road? You might see birds or other small animals eating it. When an animal dies, it's eaten by other animals. These animals are known as *scavengers*. Then, it's time for decomposers to spring into action. **Bacteria**, mushrooms, and worms are examples of decomposers. They break down the nutrients that are left in dead plants and animals. They return them to the soil. Those nutrients become food for plants to use—and the food chain begins again.

The Brown Food Chain

Green food chains start with living plants. But less than 10 percent of plants are eaten while they are alive. Most plants are eaten after they die. This dead material fuels the brown food chain. The brown food chain fuels most **ecosystems**.

The Brown Food Chain

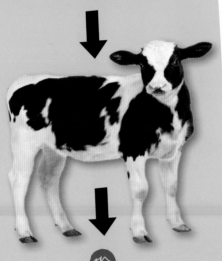

The Green Food Chain

Some predators may also be scavengers. Bears and coyotes will sometimes eat dead animals they didn't hunt themselves.

Grass may be eaten by a mouse, a rabbit, or even a snail.

A change anywhere in a food web can affect many creatures.

A cat may eat a mouse, and a coyote may eat a rabbit.

ENERGY
ENERGY
ENERGY
ENERGY
ENERGY
ENERGY
ENERGY

Weaving the Web

Plants and animals rely on one another to live. In an ecosystem, each living thing is part of many different food chains. The food chains crisscross and overlap. When you look at all the connected food chains, you end up with something that looks more like a web than a chain.

One light touch can set a whole spiderweb shaking. Food webs work the same way. A small change in one area of the web can change the whole ecosystem. Food webs show how each plant and animal is important.

ENERGY

ENERGY

A bird may eat a snail.

How Does Your Garden Grow?

Consider a simple garden. If an animal or plant in the food chain is threatened, it affects the entire garden.

What will happen if one living thing becomes **endangered**? Think of it as a woven blanket. If you pull out just one thread, the whole blanket can unravel. It is the same thing with an ecosystem. The loss of just one species can unravel the whole thing.

Long ago, hundreds of thousands of wolves roamed the United States. They hunted elk, deer, and moose. The wolves kept the numbers of those animals under control. But wolves became a threat. And humans began hunting them. Before long, wolves became an endangered species.

Before

balanced elk population

With the wolves almost gone, the number of elk was out of *p1* control. That meant the willow trees the elk grazed on were now in short supply. Fewer trees meant there was no food or shelter for songbirds. Songbirds eat mosquitos. But with the birds dying, the number of mosquitos began growing. And nobody wanted that!

Great beasts such as the sabertooth cat roamed the planet during the Ice Age before dying out.

After

increased elk population

19

Most endangered species aren't as regal as the wolf or the sabertooth cat. But they are just as important. The freshwater mussel is not much to look at. But it plays a key role in its ecosystem. It lives in North American lakes and rivers. The mussel is a food source for many kinds of life. Raccoons, otters, and herons are a few of the animals that eat them. Mussels also clean the water they live in. They make the ecosystem better for other species of fish, bugs, and worms that live there.

Extinction can have a ripple effect. When one animal dies out, others may soon follow.

Before

But the mussel is in trouble. Most of the 300 species of mussels are threatened. Experts think pollution is killing them. Toxins in the runoff from farms and cities are getting into the water they live in. This puts the entire ecosystem in danger.

New species of plants and animals are being discovered all the time, so experts aren't sure exactly how many there are. But they estimate that between 200 and 100,000 species become **extinct** every year.

After

Risk Factors

It's possible that any plant or animal could become extinct. But some living things are at higher risk than others. Plants and animals struggle to survive when:

- they live in a small area.
- there are not many of them left alive.
- they take a long time to grow and reproduce.

freshwater mussels

Rewilding

Some scientists argue that we can restore ecosystems if we make space for them. They look for land that is not being used. Then, they bring in key species. They try to undo some of the damage that has been done. In time, these areas can become wild again. This practice is called *rewilding.*

These scientists study the remains of an animal in the Netherlands. It may be the first wolf found in the country in 150 years.

The loss of wolves in an ecosystem can be devastating. Their reintroduction during rewilding can turn an ecosystem around. In 1995, 41 wolves were reintroduced into Yellowstone National Park. Their presence changed the ecosystem. Soon, there were less deer in the park. That allowed more plants to grow. Birds and beavers began to return. Ducks, frogs, and more fish followed. The wolves ate the coyotes. That meant more rabbits and mice could survive. And that provided more food for eagles and hawks. The park became a richer, more alive place.

A New Approach

In the past, scientists tried taking away or adding species over and over to ecosystems. Rewilding is different. Scientists study an ecosystem. They add essential animals to the environment. And then, humans step back and let nature take over.

Yellowstone is now home to over 400 wolves!

Where Do You Fit In?

So where do you fit into the food web?

Some people think that humans are at the top of the food chain. That is because nothing hunts humans. But that's only true today. Long ago, humans were hunted by large predators.

Experts say we are closer to the middle of the food chain. This is because we eat a mix of plants and animals. Only carnivores are considered to be at the top of the food chain. They don't have any predators. Whales, tigers, and polar bears are at the top.

A Way of Life

Instead of eating animals that eat plants, some people choose to eat only the plants. These people are *vegetarians*.

But humans can play another role, too. There are many things humans do that can harm the delicate balance of food webs. For instance, farmers kill bugs that eat their crops. But those bugs may be the main food source for a type of bird. If the bird doesn't have that bug to eat, that species of bird may start dying. It may even become extinct. The animals that rely on that bird for food may then be threatened, too. The loss of one type of bug can disrupt the balance of an entire food web. The same thing can happen when humans hunt or fish too many of one animal.

Shh!

Studies show that the sounds humans make with traffic and machines can damage ecosystems. Birds and other animals often change the way they act around loud noises. Even plants appear affected by loud noises.

Change is natural. Many of the threats to food webs come from nature. Natural disasters, such as floods or wildfires, can kill many animals. But most of the threats to food webs come from humans. Our actions affect all the living things around us. And scientists are just beginning to see how we are all connected. In big and small ways, every plant, animal, boy, and girl makes a difference. Whether it's a gooey glob of bacteria or a wild monkey, every creature plays a role.

It is up to us to protect our planet. It's our home. And it is the home of every other creature on it. The web of life will always continue if we maintain balance.

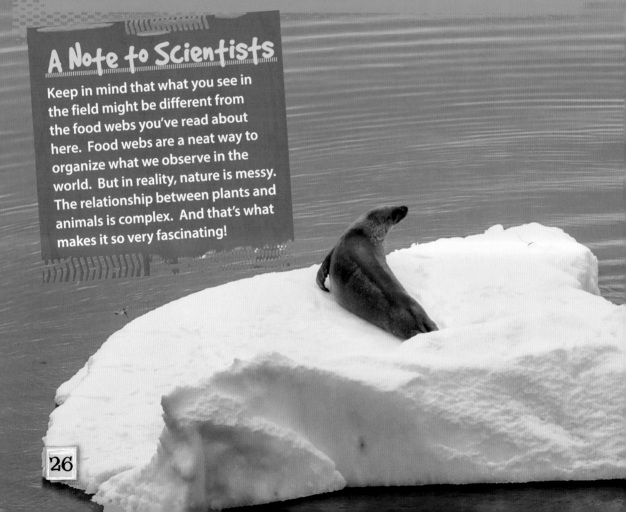

A Note to Scientists

Keep in mind that what you see in the field might be different from the food webs you've read about here. Food webs are a neat way to organize what we observe in the world. But in reality, nature is messy. The relationship between plants and animals is complex. And that's what makes it so very fascinating!

Don't feed wild animals. It makes them rely on humans for food.

Don't release pets into the wild. They may not survive, and it could disrupt the ecosystem.

Don't litter. Animals can get sick or die from eating our trash.

Do plant trees and bushes that are native to your area. Trees clean the air and create homes for animals.

Do educate others! Write letters to decision makers so they are aware of the needs of wildlife in your area.

Do volunteer at or visit a national park. You can understand the importance of every living thing if you see it yourself.

MAKE A DIFFERENCE

Think Like a Scientist

How can a change in one part of a food web affect the entire web? Experiment and find out!

What to Get

- craft sticks
- glue
- shoe box, tray, or other small box

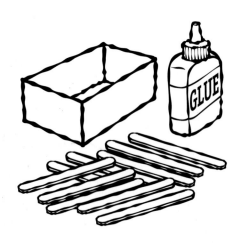

What to Do

1. Glue three craft sticks together to make a long stick. Your long stick represents producers. Make six long sticks.

2. Glue two craft sticks together to make a medium stick. Your medium stick represents primary consumers. Make seven medium sticks.

3. Place the producers across the box. Make sure they cross each other and that no sticks fall inside the box.

4. Place the primary consumers on top of the producers. Make sure none of the sticks fall into the box.

5. Use individual craft sticks to represent secondary consumers. Place these sticks on top of the primary consumers.

6. Remove one producer. What happens when one producer is removed?

7. Remove two more producers. What happens now? What does this show about the links between the animals in the food web?

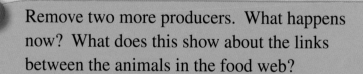
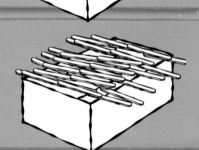

Glossary

bacteria—tiny organisms that break down dead plants and animals

carnivore—an animal that eats meat

decomposers—living things that feed on and break down dead plants or animals

ecosystems—everything that exists in particular environments

endangered—used to describe an animal or plant that is at risk of completely dying out

energy—power that can be used to do something

extinct—no longer existing

herbivores—animals that only eat plants

omnivore—an animal that eats both plants and animals

organisms—living things

primary consumers—living things that only eat producers

producers—living things that make their own food

scavengers—animals that feed on dead or decaying animals

secondary consumer—an animal that eats primary consumers

species—groups of animals or plants that are similar and can produce young animals or plants

Index

Your Turn!

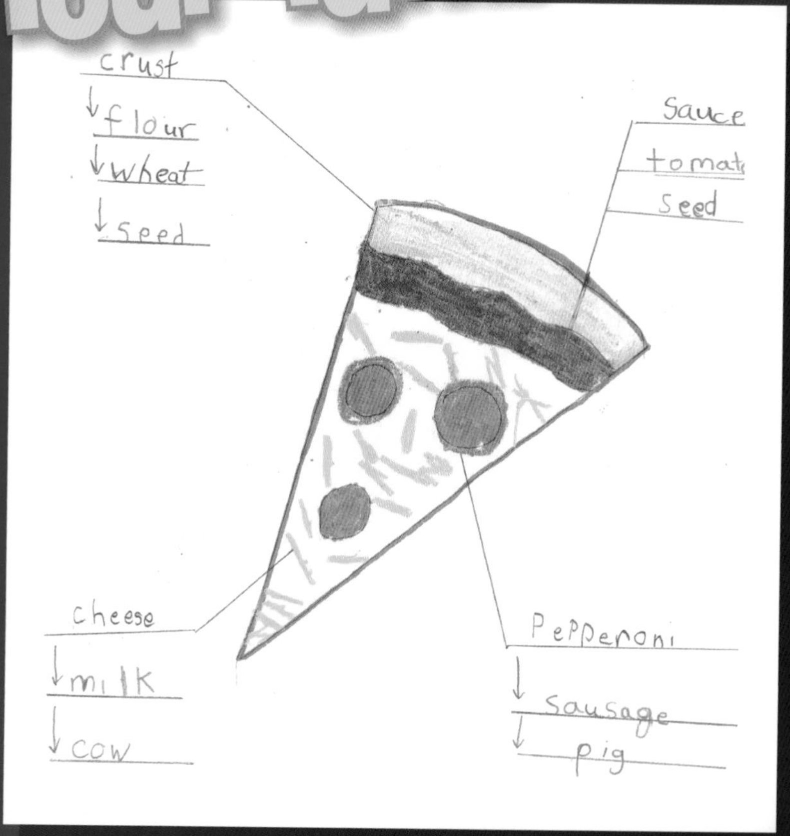

crust
flour
wheat
seed
Sauce
tomat
Seed
cheese
milk
cow
Pepperoni
sausage
pig

What's Your Web?

Make a list of the foods you eat most often. Then, break those foods down into their raw ingredients. Draw arrows from each ingredient to show all the other animals and plants that play a part in that ingredient getting to your plate. Can you find where the sun's energy goes in each food chain?